Scariest Places on Earth

TRANSYLVANIA

By Ethan Weingarten

Gareth Stevens
PUBLISHING

Please visit our website, www.garethstevens.com. For a free color catalog of all our high-quality books, call toll free 1-800-542-2595 or fax 1-877-542-2596.

Library of Congress Cataloging-in-Publication Data

Weingarten, Ethan.
Transylvania / by Ethan Weingarten.
p. cm. – (The scariest places on Earth)
Includes index.
ISBN 978-1-4824-1162-1 (pbk.)
ISBN 978-1-4824-1163-8 (6-pack)
ISBN 978-1-4824-1161-4 (library binding)
1. Haunted places – Romania – Transylvania – Juvenile literature. 2. Transylvania (Romania) – Miscellanea – Juvenile literature. 3. Vampires – Romania – Transylvania – Juvenile literature. I. Weingarten, Ethan. II. Title.
BF1472.R6 W45 2015
133.109498–d23

First Edition

Published in 2015 by
Gareth Stevens Publishing
111 East 14th Street, Suite 349
New York, NY 10003

Copyright © 2015 Gareth Stevens Publishing

Designer: Katelyn E. Reynolds
Editor: Therese Shea

Photo credits: Cover, p. 1 Paul Biris/Flickr/Getty Images; cover, pp. 1–24 (background texture) Eky Studio/Shutterstock.com; cover, pp. 1–24 (creepy design elements) Dmitry Natashin/Shutterstock.com; p. 5 mythja/Shutterstock.com; p. 7 (photo) Christian Draghici/Shutterstock.com; p. 7 (map) Andrein/Wikipedia.com; p. 9 Apic/Hulton Archive/Getty Images; p. 11 DeAgostini/Getty Images; p. 12 The British Library/Robana/Getty Images; p. 13 Emi Cristea/Shutterstock.com; p. 15 Mikadun/Shutterstock.com; p. 17 Dumitrescu Ciprian-Florin/Shutterstock.com; p. 19 Hulton Archive/Getty Images; p. 21 Doug Pearson/AWL Images/Getty Images.

Printed in the United States of America

CPSIA compliance information: Batch #CS15GS: For further information contact Gareth Stevens, New York, New York at 1-800-542-2595.

CONTENTS

Words in the glossary appear in **bold** type the first time they are used in the text.

TERRIFYING TRANSYLVANIA?

When many people think of Transylvania, they think of spooky castles, creepy bats, and—most of all—vampires! There are so many different stories about vampires. Most agree that vampires are dead people who suck the blood of the living. Some tales say they only hunt their victims at night. Others say that sunlight burns vampires.

Some of the original stories, or legends, of vampires come from the part of Romania called Transylvania. Let's find out what happened there to **inspire** such tales.

FRIGHTENING OR FUN?

Vampire legends have inspired stories of other blood-sucking creatures. Chupacabras are legendary creatures that are said to drink the blood of livestock!

Because vampires are dead, some tales say they sleep in coffins.

WHERE IS IT?

Transylvania is a **region** located in the central part of Romania, a country in eastern Europe. To the north and east are the Carpathian Mountains. The Transylvanian Alps are to the south, and the Bihor Mountains are to the west.

Transylvania has a long and sometimes bloody history. It was part of Hungary from the eleventh to the fifteenth centuries. Then, Transylvanian princes ruled their land for more than 100 years until Hungary regained control in the 1600s. Romania took over Transylvania in the early twentieth century.

6

Transylvania

ROMANIA

The first time Transylvania appeared in
written records was in the twelfth century.

DRACULA!

Dracula as most people know him isn't a real person from Transylvanian history. He's the evil main character in the book *Dracula*, which was written by Bram Stoker in 1897. However, Stoker based his bloodthirsty **villain** on a real-life Transylvanian prince from the 1400s named Vlad III.

Vlad's father was called Vlad Dracul. *Dracul* means "dragon" in Romanian. Vlad Dracul ruled the area of Transylvania called Walachia (wah-LAY-kee-uh). When Vlad III was a young man, his father sent him to live with the **Ottoman** ruler as a promise Vlad Dracul would be loyal.

Vlad III was often called Vlad Dracula, or "son of the dragon."

VLAD
THE IMPALER

When Vlad III returned to his home in Walachia 6 years later, he found that his father and older brother had been killed by nobles. He fought for the next 8 years against the Ottoman Empire to rule Walachia.

Vlad became known for his **viciousness** in battle. He **impaled** his enemies, leaving their dead bodies on **stakes** in the ground. This was meant to scare those opposing him. Some say he killed thousands this way.

BRAN CASTLE

People think *Dracula* author Bram Stoker learned about Vlad's vicious nature and decided to borrow his nickname "Dracula." Stoker definitely had a real Transylvanian castle in mind as he wrote about the vampire Dracula's castle.

Stoker described a castle built on a rock that towered over the valley below. That building is still standing. It's called Bran Castle. While Vlad Dracula never lived there, he was imprisoned at Bran Castle by the Hungarian king for 2 months in 1462.

Bran Castle was built in 1377. Even though Dracula never lived there, many people call it "Dracula's Castle."

13

HUNYADI CASTLE

Bran Castle isn't the only castle connected to the legend of Vlad the Impaler. A beautiful **fortress** in the city of Hunedoara (hoo-nay-DWAHR-ah) is said to be the scary place where Vlad Dracul, Dracula's father, was jailed by a man named John Hunyadi. Interestingly, Hunyadi later took Vlad Dracula under his protection.

The castle doesn't look today as it did in the 1400s. It has been rebuilt a number of times after a series of fires. Its numerous towers and stone carvings draw many visitors each year.

This fortress has many names. People call it Hunyadi
Castle, Hunyad Castle, Hunedoara Castle, and Corvin Castle.

15

POENARI CASTLE

There's not much left of Poenari (poy-uh-NAHR-ee) Castle near the town of Târgoviște (tuhr-GOH-veesh-tuh), but many people still visit its **ruins**. That's because this place, too, is connected to Vlad Dracula. In fact, Vlad actually lived there and used it as his fortress.

If you plan on visiting, make sure you're in shape. The castle was built into a cliff, and you have to walk up 1,480 steps to reach it! Vlad probably chose it because it was a good place to look out for approaching enemies.

FRIGHTENING OR FUN?

A few legends say that Vlad Dracula forced the townspeople to work on his fortress. Some were made to work until they fell down dead.

Earthquakes brought down parts of Poenari Castle over the years.

17

STRIGOI

Even though Vlad Dracula was a fierce warrior, he didn't suck blood that we know of. Where did that idea come from? Some villages in Transylvania have stories of vampires called *strigoi* (stree-GOY).

A *strigoi* was described as a human spirit who comes back from the dead to steal food and play tricks. It's invisible at first. However, it later becomes visible and begins sucking blood from people's hearts! If townspeople thought a dead person had become a *strigoi*, they dug up the body and burned it—or ran a spike through it!

18

OTHER WORDS FOR VAMPIRE

strigoi — Romania

vrykolakas — Greece

vampyyri — Finland

vampir — Germany

vampyr — Sweden

pijavica — Croatia

ma cà rồng — Vietnam

upyr — Russia

In other parts of eastern Europe, *strigoi* are called *vampir* or *vampyr.*

A DIFFERENT SIDE OF TRANSYLVANIA

Since the legends of Vlad the Impaler and *strigoi* are so scary, you might think Transylvania is a frightening place. However, visitors can see pretty towns that look much like they did in **medieval** times. The people there take great pride in their home and their way of life. There are celebrations with colorful clothes and dancing.

Visitors may go to Transylvania because of the terrifying tales of Dracula, but they're charmed by the Transylvania of today.

Brasov is a colorful city in Transylvania near the Carpathian Mountains.

21

GLOSSARY

crossroad: the place where two roads cross each other

earthquake: a shaking of the ground caused by the movement of Earth's crust

fortress: a building or group of buildings that are protected against attack

impale: to cause a pointed object to go into or through something or someone

inspire: to cause someone to want to do something

medieval: having to do with the Middle Ages, a time in European history from about 500 to 1500

Ottoman: relating to the Turkish empire begun in the late thirteenth century in western Asia. It ended in 1922.

region: a large area of land that has features that make it different from nearby areas of land

ruins: the remaining pieces of something that was destroyed

stake: a pointed stick or post that is pushed into the ground

viciousness: the state of being dangerous and intending to do harm

villain: a person who does bad things

FOR MORE INFORMATION

Books

Cohen, Robert Z. *Transylvania: Birthplace of Vampires*. New York, NY: Rosen Central, 2012.

Indovino, Shaina Carmel. *Transylvania and Beyond: Vampires & Werewolves in Old Europe*. Broomall, PA: Mason Crest Publishers, 2011.

Von Finn, Denny. *Transylvania*. Minneapolis, MN: Bellwether Media, 2013.

Websites

Photo Gallery: Transylvania
travel.nationalgeographic.com/travel/countries/romania-transylvania-photos-traveler/
See pictures of the real Transylvania.

Transylvania, Romania
www.romaniatourism.com/transylvania.html
Learn about places to explore in Transylvania. Click on links to learn more about the actual Dracula.

INDEX